Color & Learn Easy SPANISH PHRASES FOR KIDS

Roz Fulcher

Te quiero.
teh kee-**eh**-roh

Dover Publications, Inc.
Mineola, New York

This handy book will have you speaking Spanish in no time! More than sixty illustrated pages include commonly used words and phrases in both Spanish and English. Below each Spanish word or phrase you'll find its pronunciation. A syllable that is **boldfaced** should be stressed.

Whether it's just for fun, for travel, or to have a conversation with a friend or relative, you'll find out how to talk about the weather, tell what you'd like at mealtime, and many other helpful phrases—and you can color while you learn!

Bibliographical Note

Color & Learn Easy Spanish Phrases for Kids is a new work, first published by Dover Publications, Inc., in 2015.

International Standard Book Number

ISBN-13: 978-0-486-79759-5
ISBN-10: 0-486-79759-7

Manufactured in the United States by LSC Communications
79759707   2018
www.doverpublications.com

Good morning.

Hello.   Good-bye.

See you later.

What's your name?

My name is _____.

Es mi
ess mee

1. madre
mah-dreh

2. padre
pah-dreh

3. hermana
ehr-**mah**-nah

4. hermano
ehr-**mah**-noh

This is my   1. Mother   2. Father
               3. Sister   4. Brother

How old are you?   I am _____ years old.

I'm allergic to nuts/eggs.

I love you.

What's for breakfast?   1. Cereal

2. pan tostado
pahn tohs-**tah**-doh

3. huevos
weh-bohs

2. Toast   3. Eggs

It's time for lunch. I want. . . 1. a sandwich

2. un yogur
oon yoh-**goor**

3. una hamburguesa
oo-nah ahm-boor-**geh**-sah

2. Yogurt   3. Hamburger

I'm hungry! What's for dinner?

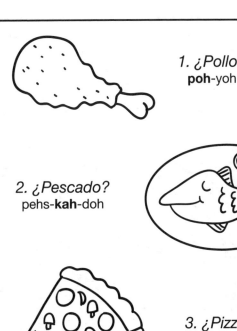

1. ¿Pollo?
poh-yoh

2. ¿Pescado?
pehs-**kah**-doh

3. ¿Pizza?
peet-sah

1. Chicken?   2. Fish?   3. Pizza?

What's for dessert?

1. helado
eh-**lah**-doh

2. fruta
froo-tah

3. galletas
gah-**yeh**-tahs

1. Ice cream   2. Fruit   3. Cookies

I like to . . .   1. Read   2. Dance

4. pasear en bicicleta
pah-seh-**ahr** ehn bee-see-**kleh**-tah

3. dibujar
dee-boo-**hahr**

3. Draw   4. Bike

1. I'm sorry.   2. Don't worry.

3. It's okay.

Can you help me, please? I'm lost.

Merry Christmas!

¡Feliz Año Nuevo!

feh-**lees ah**-nyoh **nweh**-boh!

Happy New Year!

This is delicious! I'd like some more.

Where are you from?   I am from _____.

Los días de la semana.

los **dee**-ahs deh lah seh-**mah**-nah

Monday

lunes
loo-nehs

Tuesday

martes
mahr-tehs

Wednesday

miercoles
mee-**ehr**-koh-lehs

Days of the week

Thursday *jueves*
hweh-behs

Friday *viernes*
bee-**ehr**-nehs

Saturday *sábado*
sah-bah-doh

Sunday *domingo*
doh-**meen**-goh

Months

July
julio
hoo-lee-yoh

August
agosto
ah-**gohs**-toh

September
septiembre
sehp-tee-**ehm**-breh

October
octubre
ohk-**too**-breh

November
noviembre
noh-bee-**ehm**-breh

December
diciembre
dee-see-**ehm**-breh

Los números
lohs **noo**-meh-rohss

uno
oo-noh

dos
dohs

tres
trehs

cuatro
kwah-troh

cinco
seen-koh

Numbers

seis
sehs

siete
see-**eh**-teh

ocho
oh-choh

nueve
noo-**eh**-beh

diez
dee-**ehs**

Los colores
lohs koh-**loh**-rehs

Green
verde
behr-deh

Red
rojo
roh-hoh

Blue
azul
ah-**sool**

Colors

Yellow
amarillo
ah-mah-**ree**-yoh

Colors

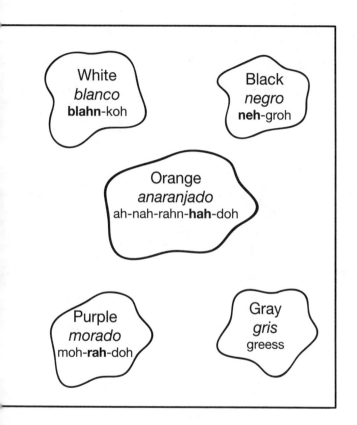

White
blanco
blahn-koh

Black
negro
neh-groh

Orange
anaranjado
ah-nah-rahn-**hah**-doh

Purple
morado
moh-**rah**-doh

Gray
gris
greess

1. Let's go to the park!
2. Awesome idea!

1. How much does it cost?

2. It's one dollar.

Let's go to the beach! I will get my . . .

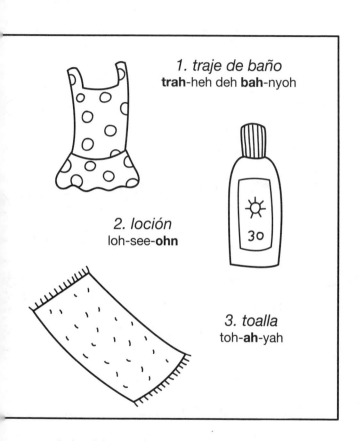

1. traje de baño
trah-heh deh **bah**-nyoh

2. loción
loh-see-**ohn**

3. toalla
toh-**ah**-yah

1. bathing suit   2. lotion   3. towel

Please.

Thank you.   You're welcome.

It's raining. I'm taking my . . .

1. umbrella   2. raincoat

Could you speak more slowly?

It's hot today. I'll wear . . .

1. una camiseta
oo-nah kah-mee-**seh**-tah

2. unos pantalones cortos
oo-nohs pahn-tah-**loh**-nehs
kohr-tohs

3. unas sandalias
oo-nahs sahn-**dah**-lee-ahs

1. a T-shirt   2. shorts   3. sandals

It's snowing! I need . . .

2. mis guantes
mees **gwahn**-tehs

1. mi bufanda
mee boo-**fahn**-dah

3. mis botas
mees **boh**-tahs

4. mi abrigo
mee ah-**bree**-goh

1. my scarf   2. my gloves
3. my boots   4. my coat

I'm cold. I need . . .

1. un suéter
oon **sweh**-tehr

2. una manta
oo-nah **mahn**-tah

3. una chaqueta
oo-nah chah-**keh**-tah

1. a sweater   2. a blanket   3. a jacket

Do you speak English?

Sorry, I don't understand.

I'm thirsty. I want . . .

1. agua
ah-gwah

2. jugo
hoo-goh

3. leche
leh-cheh

1. water   2. juice   3. milk

Excuse me. Where is the nearest . . .

1. el restaurante
ehl rehs-tahw-**rahn**-teh

2. la parada de autobús
lah pah-**rah**-dah deh ahw-toh-**boos**

3. el metro
ehl **meh**-troh

1. restaurant?   2. bus stop?

3. subway?

Do you have a pet?   I have a . . .

1. *perro*
peh-roh

2. *gato*
gah-toh

3. *pez*
pays

4. *pájaro*
pah-hah-roh

5. *hámster*
ahm-stehr

1. dog   2. cat   3. fish
4. bird   5. hamster

Happy birthday! My birthday is in

_____.

1. *ver la televisión*
behr lah
teh-leh-bee-see-**ohn**

2. *ir al cine*
eer ahl **see**-neh

3. *salir afuera*
sah-**leer** ah-**fweh**-rah

¿Puedo . . .?
pweh-doh

Can I . . . 1. Watch TV?
2. Go to a movie?
3. Go outside?

Where is the bathroom?

1. abuela
ah-**bway**-lah

2. abuelo
ah-**bway**-loh

3. tía
tee-ah

4. tío
tee-oh

5. prima
pree-mah

6. primo
pree-moh

1. Grandma
2. Grandpa
3. Aunt
4. Uncle
5. Cousin (girl)
6. Cousin (boy)

I don't feel well. My . . . 1. throat   2. head
                          3. stomach . . . (hurts)

I'm tired. Time for bed.

Good night.